# Concrete Siberia

**by**
**Zupagrafika**

Photography:

Alexander Veryovkin

ZUPA
GRA
FiKA

## Contents

# Push eastwards:
# Soviet urbanisation in Siberia

Norilsk is an exceptional city by any measure. Situated 300 km above the Arctic circle, the city is covered with snow for up to nine months of the year and, on average, it will endure more than a hundred snowstorms annually. The polar night hides the sun for 45 days. In *The Game of Thrones*' coordinate system Norilsk is far beyond the Wall – and for half of the year it feels like the Night King is having a party. Its existential purpose lies deep in the earth: Norilsk's mines supply 35% of the world's palladium, 25% of platinum and 20% of nickel.

What strikes you, on visiting Norilsk, is that despite its extreme climate the planning and architecture resemble any other city built in Soviet times. There is a main street named after Lenin. The main square is formed of Stalinist buildings, dressed in columns. Most of its urban fabric is woven from prefabricated apartment blocks. This mediocrity in the face of its specific environmental features is puzzling. Why was a city beyond the Arctic circle designed like any other industrial city in the USSR? In 1958, the Canadian city of Frobisher Bay, announced an extraordinary plan to build a city under a dome. The design made sense given the climate conditions, similar to those of Norilsk. At the time, architects believed new technologies and engineering solutions would make it possible to build futuristic cities in remote areas. This was not the case. The envisioned dome never materialised.

The Soviet approach to developing its territories was based on prefabricated construction, the exact opposite of the Frobisher Bay's sci-fi dreams. The ambition of Soviet urban planners was on developing a universal technological approach that could be applied to any place on the planet – even Norilsk – not on designing architectural marvels. Today the population of the city is around 180,000. Its mines are thriving.

Prefabrication and serialisation became the key premises for Soviet urban development when Khrushchev came to power. For Siberia, it meant a new wave of colonisation.

During Stalin's rule development of the region was, to a great extent, determined by production plans, namely the optimisation of extraction and processing of natural resources. Stalinist architecture was concerned less with accommodating people's needs than with promoting an ideological vision. Following Hannah Arendt, Stalinist architecture in remote regions functioned as antennae that received and reproduced images of central power.

# 'Prefabrication and serialisation became the key premises for Soviet urban development when Khrushchev came to power. For Siberia, it meant a new wave of colonisation.'

Khrushchev's shift to prefabrication meant architecture was no longer about reproducing the image of power but about replicating a standard of urban life across the Soviet empire. The new form of development focused on building and peopling cities. Workers were not just forced to move, they were attracted to Siberian cities by the promise of a flat in one of the prefabricated blocks. From the beginning of Khrushchev's era to the fall of the USSR, the populations of the cities featured in this book more than doubled. The plan was a success.

In addition to prefabricated apartment blocks, public facilities were built in accord with the narrow Soviet understanding of what public life should be. Typification was in use here, as well as for prefab apartment blocks. Circuses in Krasnoyarsk and Omsk were built following identical designs. Many regions were provided with plans by Moscow-based design institutes. The role of local architects was to implement the designs. The spectacular Musical Theatre in Omsk, which resembles a ski-jump, was designed in Moscow at the TSNIIEP Mezentseva (ЦНИИЭП зрелищных зданий и спортивных сооружений) Institute which produced plans for theatres and sport facilities across the USSR.

Shifting power dynamics between central and regional authorities opened a new chapter for local architecture since Khrushchev's leadership. Regional authorities were no longer interested in just building designs from Moscow; they sought to develop their own.

Areg Demirkhanov moved to Krasnoyarsk from Novosibirsk, the city with the strongest architectural school in Siberia. The public buildings he designed, including the Lenin Museum, City Hall and the Philharmonic, define the character of Krasnoyarsk's urban landscape to this day. Many talented architects were recruited to work in Siberian cities, including Vladimir Pavlov who moved to Irkutsk from Leningrad. With dozens of completed projects, he created a regional version of the late modernist style in Irkutsk.

Sometimes regional design stood in direct opposition to Moscow. Central Stadium in Krasnoyarsk was meant to be a replica of Moscow's Lokomotiv Stadium. Alexander Grishin, the director of the Grazhdanproekt Institute who was responsible for the project, shelved the project plans from Moscow and constructed an innovative design by a young architect from Leningrad, Vitaly Orekhov, instead. The building's unveiling caused a scandal, however, Orekhov's architecture gained many admirers. His stadium was one of the first brutalist buildings in Krasnoyarsk and Grishin had managed to outwit central power. In the end, what is the point of living thousands of kilometres from the capital if it does not gain you some freedom?

**Konstantin Budarin**
Independent writer and researcher based in Moscow

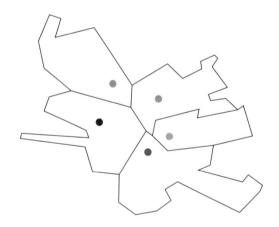

| Kirovsky | ● | 12, 13, 27, 28, 29 |
| Leninsky | ● | 26 |
| Oktyabrsky | ● | 16 |
| Sovetsky | ● | 22 |
| Tsentralny | ● | 10, 11, 14, 15, 17, 18, 19, 20, 21, 23, 24, 25 |

# Omsk

A centre of anti-Bolshevism during the Russian Civil War, and
the site of Dostoyevsky's exile, Omsk has been known, since
the 1950s, as an oil city. The construction of Russia's largest
oil-refinery there during the Soviet era largely defined its urban
landscape. The Moscow Giprogor Institute planned the city's
northward expansion along the Irtysh River and onto its left
bank, creating Novo-Omsk, where new units would house
the fast-growing population. In the early 1960s, 400 wooden
barracks built for refinery workers in the former Stalin District
were demolished and some 4,500 families were relocated to
concrete panel block apartments. The settlement, nicknamed
Oil Town, was the largest, most comfortable and most
desirable microrayon in Omsk. Soon, brick tower blocks and
geometrical living quarters made of concrete Khrushchevka
and Brezhnevka started to appear en masse, keeping pace with
the plastic, rubber and detergent plants springing up around
the northern districts. Today, Sovetsky and Kirovsky still house
the majority of the city's inhabitants and maintain an aesthetic
dialogue with concrete memorials of the Soviet era, such as the
Pushkin National Library, or the Opera House which tower over
Tsentralny District.

State Musical Theatre | Architects: D. Lurie, N. Struzhin, N. Belousova | Built: 1982 | Tsentralny District

Victor Blinov monument (Soviet Hockey League player and Olympic and World Ice Hockey champion)
ul. Dekabristov | Tsentralny District

Tiled panel block in ul. Lukashevicha  |  Built: mid-1980s  |  Kirovsky District

◁◁

Blinov Sports and Concerts Complex
Built: 1986  |  Architects: Omskgrazhdanproekt,
led by Mikhail Khakhaev  |  Tsentralny District

△

Nine-storey apartment block
Series 090  |  Built: 1984
Oktyabrsky District

16

Brezhnevka in ul. Zvezdova  |  Built: 1986  |  Tsentralny District

◁◁

TETs-5 electric power station
Tsentralny District

△

Ul. Irkutskaya  |  Built: 1970s
Amursky, Tsentralny District

Former Irtysh Sports and Concert Complex (From 2001 Blinov Sports and Concerts Complex)
Tsentralny District

Twelve-storey apartment block in ul. Krasny Put  |  Built: 1975  |  Sovetsky District

State Regional Research Library, named after Alexander Pushkin  |  Architects: G. Ivanovna Naritsina,
Y. Alekseevich Zakharov  |  Built: 1995  |  Tsentralny District

Housing estate from the 1970s on the left bank of the Irtysh River  |  Kirovsky District

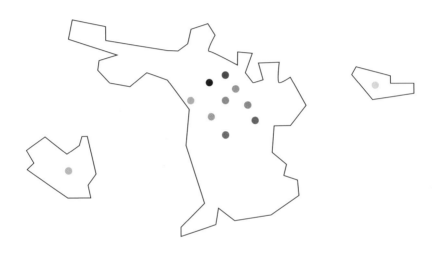

| | | |
|---|---|---|
| Microrayon 2-3 | ● | 35 |
| Microrayon 4 | ● | 51 |
| Microrayon 5 | ● | 43, 48, 49 |
| Microrayon 7 | ● | 58 |
| Microrayon 8 | ● | 60, 61 |
| Microrayon 10 | ● | 36, 37 |
| Microrayon 11 | ● | 34, 40 |
| Microrayon 15 | ● | 54 |
| Nadezhda | ● | 32, 33 |
| Oganer | ● | 38, 39, 44, 45, 46, 47, 52, 53, 55, 59 |
| Zheleznodorozhny | ● | 42 |

# Norilsk

Surrounded by clouds of sulphur fumes and rows of colourful prefabricated panel blocks protecting its city centre from the icy wind is the subarctic city of Norilsk. Like other Soviet-era monotowns (or Моногород), it was designed around a single industry in a remote part of the Soviet Union. In this case, the city was planned around Nickel Norilsk, the world's largest extractor of nickel, palladium and platinum, which employed the majority of its inhabitants. Its perennially frozen ground made urban development particularly challenging. The first wooden houses were erected by labourers from the Norillag gulag in 1935. When the gulag closed in 1957, a local 'house factory' started to mass-produce prefabricated panels for a five-storey Khrushchevka providing locals with the city's first decent, climate-proof housing. To protect the permafrost from heat emitted by housing units, all the blocks were erected on reinforced concrete piles frozen into the subarctic soil. Thanks to this method, Norilsk began to grow up and outwards. Incorporating the nearby towns of Talnakh and Kayerkan, it had become the largest Arctic municipality constructed on permafrost by the 1980s. However, not all the houses on concrete legs stood the test of time.

◁◁

Nadezhda Metallurgical Plant  |  Built: 1979
Road connecting Norilsk Central District
with Nadezhda complex

△

Nine-storey panel block in ul. Komsomolskaya
Series 111-112  |  Built: 1983
Microrayon 11

Ploshchad Metallurgov, 27. Series 111-112 | Built: 1984 | Microrayon 2-3

Microrayon 10, as seen from ul. Krasnoyarskaya | Tsentralny District

Molodyozhny proyezd. Series 1-464-82d | Built: 1970 | Microrayon 10

◁◁

Unfinished nine-storey residential blocks
in ul. Ozyornaya  |  Oganer Microrayon

△

Precast panel complex. Series 111-112
Built: 1983  |  Microrayon 11

'Nurdkamal' mosque on Lake Dolgoe and a 111–112-series panel block  |  Built: 1993  |  Tsentralny District

Bus stop along route No. 4 to Sanatorium Kindergarten | Zheleznodorozhny (former 17th Camp District)

Nine-storey panel block in ul. Laureatov. Series 111-112  |  Built: 1986  |  Microrayon 5

◁◁

'Pile fields' in Oganer
residential area. A third of
the territory is unfinished
or abandoned.

△

Oganer Microrayon was
founded in 1986 and was
intended to be an example
of a polar city.

▷▷

pp. 48-49:
Brick housing complex
in ul. Talnakhskaya. Series K69
Built: 1976  | Microrayon 5

Nine-storey panel block in Oganer Microrayon. Series 111-112 | Built: early 1990s

V.I. Lenin monument at the south entrance to Norilsk  |  Built: 1954  |  Oktyabrskaya ploshchad

Ul. Khantayskaya. City edge north  |  Built: 1981  |  Microrayon 4

Prefabricated panel blocks on concrete foundation piles | Oganer Microrayon

Norilsk Polar Theatre of Drama
named after Vl. Mayakovsky
Architects: A. Chernyshev, V. Shikhov,
V. Bolesin, A. Zakharov, V. Zesulia
Built: 1986 | Tsentralny District

Five-storey apartment block. Series 1-464M  |  Built: 1969  |  Microrayon 7

△

Unfinished 84 KOPE-N series block in
ul. Ozyornaya | Oganer Microraryon

▷▷

Ul. Laureatov nine-storey panel housing
complex | Built: 1986 | Microrayon 8

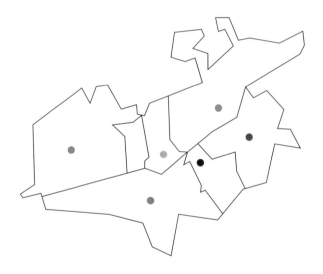

Kirovsky ● 64

Leninsky ● 66, 67, 68, 76, 78, 79, 80, 87

Oktyabrsky ● 71

Sovetsky ● 65, 69, 72, 84

Sverdlovsky ● 74, 75, 81, 82, 83, 86, 90, 91

Tsentralny ● 70, 73, 76, 77, 85, 88, 89

# Krasnoyarsk

Back in the 1930s, the Moscow Gorstroyproekt Institute drew
up a detailed urban plan for 'Greater Krasnoyarsk' along the axis
provided by the never-freezing River Yenisei. The city had just
become one of the most important industrial centres in Siberia but
lacked basic housing facilities for a mass influx of factory workers
and their families. The main goal was to replace the makeshift
wooden huts springing up around plants on the right riverbank with
decent housing units and organized urban spaces. Experimental
projects called 'cities of the future', focused on upgrading the
generally poor living standards of newcomers, were carried out
in several microrayons, such as Obraztsovo in Kirovsky District.
Today, the urban landscapes of these districts (including Leninisky,
Kirovsky and Sverdlovsky) are composed mainly of Soviet 'specials'
– concrete Khrushchevka, Brezhnevka and red-brick tower blocks
surrounded by greenery. The old town's left bank, with the adjacent
Otdykha Isle, on the other hand, offer quite a few examples of
post-war modernist and brutalist architecture at its finest. Grand
concrete designs erected between the 1960s and 1980s, such as
the striking Central Stadium or Dvorets Sporta, are the bold legacy
of young local architects Vitaly Orekhov, Areg Demirkhanov and
Eduard Panov, and display their creative take on the brutalist trends
practised in Western Europe.

Nine-storey *panelki* in Prospekt Gazety Krasnoyarskiy Rabochiy  |  Built: 1987  |  Kirovsky District

Svetlogorsky Pereulok | Microrayon Severny, Sovetsky District

◁◁ | △

Soviet decor on side elevations in
ul. Yunosti  |  Built: 1982
Leninsky District

▷

Mig-21F Plane in Prospekt Metallurgov
Housing complex  |  Built: 1980s
Sovetsky District

Central Stadium  |  Architect: V. Orekhov  |  Built: 1967  |  Otdykh Island, Tsentralny District

'Orbit' new residential complex in Oktyabrsky District, erected above the Krasnoyarsk Flour Mill
(built by gulag prisoners in 1936), as seen from Nikolayevskiy Most

Precast tiled tower block in ul. Belinskogo  |  Built: 1987  |  Sovetsky District

△

Ul. Bograda prefabricated high-rise
Built: early 1980s
Tsentralny District

▷▷

Prospekt Gazety Krasnoyarskiy Rabochiy
High-rise complex  |  Built: mid-1980s
Sverdlovsky District

Sixteen-storey apartment block in ul. Dubrovinskogo. Series 77g | Built: 1981 | Tsentralny District

Krasnoyarsk Regional Palace of Pioneers | Built: 1986 | Architects: V. Orekhov, V. Vasiliev
Mosaics: Y. Frantsiskovich | Tsentralny District

Nine-storey prefabricated panel
block in ul. Polzunova
Built: 1989
Leninsky District

△

Ten-storey housing unit in ul. 26
Bakinskikh Komissarov | Built: early
1990s | Leninsky District

▷

Fish farm on the Yaryginskaya
embankment
Sverdlovsky District

◁◁

State Circus in Prospekt Gazety Krasnoyarskiy
Rabochiy | Architects: V. Orekhov, L. Segal,
V. Mironovich | Built: 1971 | Sverdlovsky District

△

Facade detail of a 97-series large panel
residential building in ul. Belinsky
Built: 1987 | Sovetsky District

Krasnoyarsk Regional Palace of Pioneers | Built: 1986 | Archtiects: V. Orekhov, V. Vasiliev | Tsentralny District

Residential complex in Leninsky District | Built: 1981

Newton Park and Museum Centre (former Lenin Museum)  |  Architects: A. Demirkhanov, A. Bakusov, V. Korotkov,
V. Rivin  |  Built: 1987  |  Ploshchad Mira, Tsentralny District

△

Ivan Yarygin Sports Palace
Architect: V. Orekhov  |  Built: 1981
Otdykh Island, Tsentralny District

▷▷

'Siberian Convict Way' memorial complex representing
political prisoners  |  Built: 1978  |  Prospekt Gazety
Krasnoyarskiy Rabochiy,  Sverdlovsky District

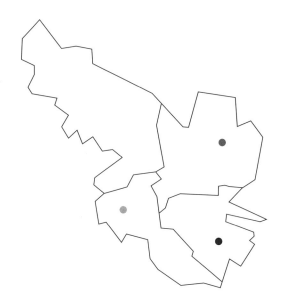

Oktyabrsky ● 98

Pravoberezhny ● 96, 97, 99

Sverdlovsky ● 94, 95, 100, 101, , 102, 103, 104, 105

# Irkutsk

The city offers an unusual retrospective of architectonic styles.
These include the iconic 'lace' wooden houses once inhabited by
those in exile, the characteristic sacral Siberian Baroque and
the pronounced constructivist and Soviet modernist legacy.
Walking around Irkutsk's central district, Oktyabrsky, one can
easily stumble upon brick and concrete residential houses such
as the Marshala Zhukova 'ship-houses' and public buildings like
the Regional Musical Theatre (whose shape invited unflattering
nicknames such as 'the crematorium' and 'the coffin'). These
were erected in Pavlov or Irkutsk Renaissance style which was
inspired by Western brutalism (although moulded to fit the newly
developed Siberian urban landscapes and severe climate).
Named after its leading and most prolific architect, Vladimir
Pavlov, the style is characterized by bold geometric forms and
solid anti-seismic building techniques and has been a distinctive
feature of the city since the 1970s.

◁◁

Irkutsk State University Dormitory no. 10
Built: 1991 | Architects: V. Pavlov, N. Belyakov,
N. Bukh, N. Zhukovsky, O. Kozlova
Universitetsky Microrayon, Sverdlovsky District

△ | ▷

Precast panel blocks in Microrayon Zelenyy
built for the Irkutsk Guards Cadet Corps of the
Strategic Missile Forces. Panel series 135
Built: 1986 | Pravoberezhny District

Regional Musical Theatre named after Nikolai Matveyevich Zagursky  |  Architects: N. Stuzhin,
A. Kudryavtsev, D. Lurie  |  Built: 1989  |  Oktyabrsky District

Pedagogical Institute Dormitory no. 1. | Architects: V. Pavlov, S. Grigoryev, V. Afanasyev
Built: 1990s | Pravoberezhny District

Izba and a nine-storey panel block | Built: 1973 | Sverdlovsky District

Series 464 block in ul. Mamina-Sibiryaka   |   Built: 1987   |   Pervomaysky Microrayon, Sverdlovsky District

△ | ▷

Terrace prefab panel blocks. Series 135 | Built: 1987
Universitetsky Microrayon, Sverdlovsky District

Residential building in ul. Ulan-Batorskaya  |  Built: 1990s  |  Universitetsky Microrayon, Sverdlovsky District

Nine-storey residential complex  |  Built: 1990s  |  Sverdlovsky District

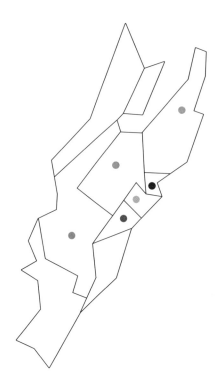

| | | |
|---|---|---|
| Gubinsky | ● | 108, 109, 110, 111, 123 |
| Oktyabrsky | ● | 119, 120, 131 |
| Promyshlenny | ● | 121, 126, 127 |
| Saysarsky | ● | 122, 124, 125, 129 |
| Stroitelny | ● | 118 |
| Tsentralny | ● | 112, 113, 115, 130 |

# Yakutsk

Extreme temperatures and omnipresent labyrinths of icicle-laden pipes are the first things to strike a visitor touching down at Mezhdunarodnyy airport and heading to the city centre through the Gagarinsky and Promyshlenny districts. The subarctic city of Yakutsk, capital of the Sakha Republic (Yakutia), lies amidst the vast empty tundra of the Far Eastern Federal District. It is accessible only by air for most of the year. Known as the coldest city in the world, its urban design is dictated by the year-long permafrost. *No digging!* is the first rule of construction. Excavation would render the permafrost unstable, causing buildings and roads to collapse due to thawing. Gas and water pipes are laid high overground, but what about buildings? Brick construction used in the 1940s did not stand the test of time. Eventually, using 12-15 metre concrete piles to keep edifices above the ground proved to be the most effective way to coexist with permafrost. Since the 1970s, concrete piles have become the city's architectural signature, supporting everything from large panel block apartments to public buildings.

Ul. Larionova prefab panel block  |  Built: late 1980s  |  202 Microrayon, Gubinsky District

*Panelki* in 202 Microrayon  |  Built: 1990s  |  Gubinsky District

◁◁
Roman Dmitriyev Embankment
Gubinsky District

△

North-Eastern Siberia Air Navigation Office
in ul. Ordzhonikidze | Tsentralny District

СЛАВЬСЯ, СТРАНА... ...ДИМСЯ ТОБОЙ!

V.I. Lenin monument in front of the Government House No. 2 | Ploshchad Lenina, Tsentralny District

Four-storey housing complex | Tuymaada Valley

Ul. Petra Alekseyeva prefabricated panel block | Built: mid-1980s | Tsentralny District

◁◁

The city dam | Built between 1958 and 1960 to block
the city channel and provide a backwater for the river
port. The pipes lead to the Yakutsk thermal power plant.

△

Dormitory of the Far-Eastern Law
Institute | Okruzhnoye Shosse,
Stroitelny District

118

Sports complex 'Triumph' | Saysary Lake, Oktyabrsky District

　Five-storey apartment block in ul. Lermontova. Series KPD 464　|　Built: 1989　|　Oktyabrsky District

Ul. Kalvitsa, Microrayon Rabochiy Gorodok  |  Built: 1982  |  Promyshlenny District

Saysary Lake view of ul. Lermontova housing complex  |  Built: 1988  |  Saysarsky District

Ul. Bogatyreva bridge over Soldatskoye Lake | Gubinsky District

◁◁

Izba and a prefab panel block in
ul. Sofronova. Series KPD 1-464 VM
Built: 1989 | Saysarsky District

△

Ploshchad Pobedy memorial of the
Great Patriotic War (1941-1945)
Built: 1975 | Promyshlenny District

126

Tank T-34, part of the Ploshchad Pobedy memorial in Promyshlenny District

Khrushchevka on the south-west edge of the city  |  Microrayon Ptitsefabrica

Road patrol service control tower | Saysarsky District

▷▷

△

Street market in ul. Lermontova
Tsentralny District

pp. 132-133: Residential blocks on concrete
piles fixed into underground permafrost.
Markha Microrayon in the Tuymaada Valley

KPD 464 precast panel block | Built: 1991 | Oktyabrsky District

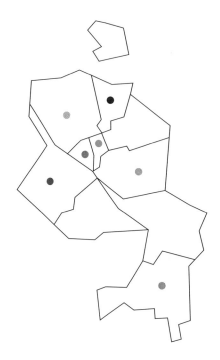

| Kalininsky | ● | 143 |
| Leninsky | ● | 146, 147 |
| Oktyabrsky | ● | 138, 139, 142, 144, 152, 153, 156, 157 |
| Sovetsky | ● | 149, 154 |
| Tsentralny | ● | 136, 145, 148, 150 |
| Zayeltsovsky | ● | 155 |
| Zheleznodorozhny | ● | 137, 140, 141, 151 |

# Novosibirsk

Under Josef Stalin Novonikolayevsk became the key industrial hub and official centre of the Siberian Region. With its mining equipment, metal and food processing plants, power station and a new name, Novosibirsk had become Siberia's fastest growing city by the 1930s. The population of the 'Siberian Chicago' skyrocketed to almost 300,000, triggering a construction boom. In the late 1930s the left bank of the Ob River (the contemporary Kirovsky and Leninsky districts) became a playground for the Giprogor's (State Institute for Town Planning) urban development plan, the Socialist City. The settlement was to be divided into industrial and residential districts with a wide green belt, embodying the Corbusian ideals of communal living and garden cities. After the most urgent housing needs were met by standardised versions of the prefabricated panel blocks erected all over the USSR, urban planners from the SibZNIIEP Institute began to design new typologies, adjusting the prefab panel construction system to Novosibirsk's climatic and topographic conditions. In the 1980s the first 97 Series nine-storey block was erected in the Leninsky District. The design, which allowed for a more functional arrangement of space in apartments, was used across the city, improving inhabitants' living conditions.

The Globus Theatre  |  Built: 1984  |  Architects: M. Starodubov, A. Sabirov  |  Tsentralny District

P-44 prefab panel estate  |  Built: 1980s  |  Zheleznodorozhny District

Facade detail of the Legislative Assembly of the Novosibirsk Region

Legislative Assembly of the Novosibirsk Region  |  Built: 1981  |  Architect: M. Pirogov  |  Oktyabrsky District

◁◁

Concrete high-rise residential block in
ul. 1905 Goda  |  Built: 1990s
Zheleznodorozhny District

△

Prefab panel residential complex in
ul. Volochayevskaya  |  Plyushchikhinsky
Microrayon, Oktyabrsky District

Civic Centre for Children in ul. Krasnykh Zor  |  Built: 1987  |  Kalininsky District

　TETs-5 electric power station  |  Built: 1985  |  Oktyabrsky District

The Globus Theatre | Built: 1984 | Architects: M. Starodubov, A. Sabirov | Tsentralny District

New residential complex in Chistaya
Sloboda Microrayon  |  Zapadnyy
Housing Estate, Leninsky District

△

Novosibirsk State Circus in ul. Chelyuskintsev
Architects: S. Gelfer, G. Naprienko, V. Kornilov
Built: 1971  |  Tsentralny District

Ten-storey apartment building. Series: 111-90 | Built: early 1990s | Nizhny Yeltsovka Microrayon, Sovetsky District

V.I. Lenin monument  in front of the Opera and Ballet Theatre  |  Ploshchad Lenina, Tsentralny District

Marins Park Hotel (former Hotel 'Novosibirsk')  |  Built: 1975  |  Architect: V. Krasovitsky  |  Zheleznodorozhny District

Large-panel residential block, series 111-97, developed at the SibZNIIEP Institute in Novosibirsk

Built: 1988 | Oktyabrsky District

Thirteen-storey tower block. Series 3424-VI-3A | Built: 1990s | Oktyabrsky District

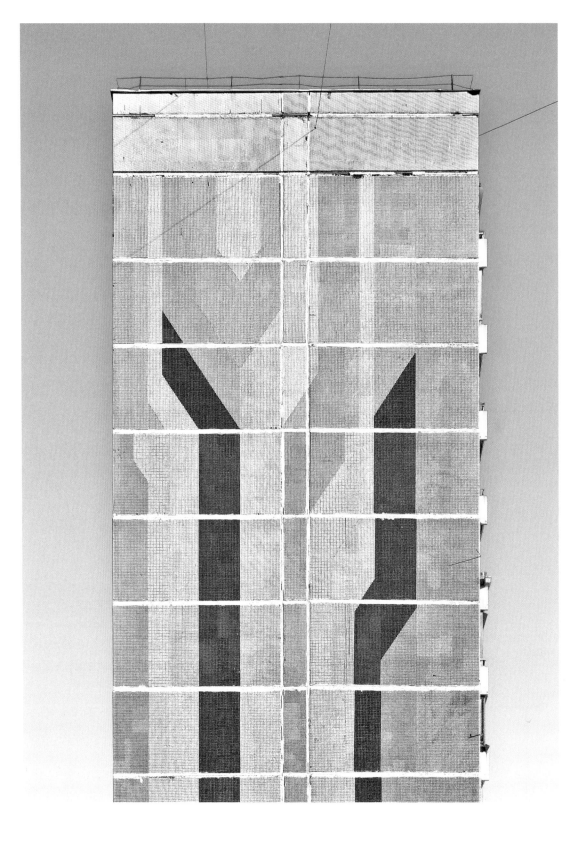

Series 1-90 apartment block in ul. Equatornaya  |  Built: 1990s  |  Nizhny Yeltsovka Microrayon, Sovetsky District

△

Yuri Gagarin portrait at Gagarinskaya
Metro Station | Opened in 1992
Zayeltsovsky District

▷▷

MZHK 'East' youth residential complex
(one of the first in the USSR)
Built: 1988 | Oktyabrsky District

# Acknowledgements

**Zupagrafika** would like to thank Alexander Veryovkin, Konstantin Budarin, Bogna Świątkowska, Maciej Kabsch, Marta & Maciej Mach, Paquita & Pepe, Kasia & Paweł, Andrés & Judit, Rita & Simón, for their help and support.

**Alexander Veryovkin** would like to thank Anastasia Makarenko, Maria Rybka, Maria Alexandrova and Juliana Semenova for their support during the shooting.

# Authors

**Zupagrafika** are David Navarro and Martyna Sobecka, an independent publisher, author and graphic design studio, established in 2012 in Poznań, Poland, celebrating modernist architecture, design and photography in a unique and playful way.

Over the last decade, David and Martyna have created, illustrated and published award-winning books exploring the post-war modernist and brutalist architecture of the former Eastern Bloc and beyond, such as *Miasto Blok-How* (2012), *Blok Wschodni* (2014) and *Blokowice* (2016). In 2015, they created the 'Brutal London' series, documenting brutalist architecture in London at risk of disappearing. The collection quickly attracted worldwide attention and was translated into

the book *Brutal London: Construct Your Own Concrete Capital* (Prestel, 2016). Zupagrafika's subsequent publications include *Brutal East* (2017), *The Constructivist* (2017), *Modern East* (2017), *Brutal Britain* (2018), *Hidden Cities* (2018), *Panelki* (2019), *Eastern Blocks* (2019), *Concrete Siberia* (2020), *Brutal Poland* (2020), and *Monotowns* (2021).

*Concrete Siberia* is a follow-up to their book *Eastern Blocks* (2019), a photographic journey through the concrete landscapes of the former Eastern Bloc. This time, Zupagrafika asked the Russian photographer Alexander Veryovkin to capture the post-war modernist architecture around the microrayons of Omsk, Krasnoyarsk, Irkutsk, Yakutsk, Norilsk and Novosibirsk.

**Alexander Veryovkin** is a photographer, born in 1987 in Leningrad (in the former USSR), currently living and working in St. Petersburg, Russia. He graduated from the Faculty of Mathematics and Mechanics at St. Petersburg

State University, majoring in astronomy. His work has been exhibited in museums and art centres in various cities including Amsterdam, Minsk, St. Petersburg and Moscow. He is also the photographer of *Monotowns* (Zupagrafika, 2021).

Texts, design and edition: David Navarro & Martyna Sobecka (Zupagrafika)

Photography: Alexander Veryovkin for Zupagrafika

Foreword: Konstantin Budarin

Cover and index images: Oganer Microrayon (Norilsk)
Foreword image: Zelenyy Microrayon (Irkutsk)

Published by Zupagrafika
Poznań, Poland. 2020

Printed in Poland
Paper from responsible sources
ISBN 978-83-950574-6-5
www.zupagrafika.com